SPORTS GREAT
HAKEEM
OLAJUWON

—*Sports Great Books*—

SPORTS GREAT HAKEEM OLAJUWON

Ron Knapp

—Sports Great Books—

ENSLOW PUBLISHERS, INC.

Bloy St. & Ramsey Ave.   P.O. Box 38
Box 777   Aldershot
Hillside, N.J. 07205   Hants GU12 6BP
U.S.A.   U.K.

Library of Congress Cataloging-in-Publication Data

Knapp, Ron.
    Sports great Hakeem Olajuwon / Ron Knapp
       p. cm. — (Sports great books)
    Includes index.
    Summary: Describes the life and career of the noted Houston
Rockets basketball player, from his childhood to the present.
    ISBN 0-89490-372-1
    1. Olajuwon, Hakeem, 1963- —Juvenile literature. 2. Basketball
players—United States—Biography—Juvenile literature.
[1. Olajuwon, Hakeem, 1963- . 2. Basketball players. 3.
Blacks—Nigeria—Biography.] I. Title. II. Series.
GV884.043K58 1992
796.323'092—dc20
[B]

                              91-41526
                                  CIP
                                    AC

Printed in the United States of America

10 9 8 7 6 5 4

Illustration Credits: Courtesy, Atlanta Hawks, p. 36; Boston Celtics, p. 49;
Mitchell Layton Photography, pp. 12, 19, 28, 35, 51, 55, 56, 60; New Jersey Nets,
p. 46; New York Knicks, p. 40; Nigerian Embassy, pp. 14, 15, 16; Sacramento
Kings, pp. 45, 54; University of Houston, pp. 8, 10, 22, 26, 30.

Cover Photo: Mitchell Layton Photography

Contents

Chapter 1

Fans called the Houston Cougars basketball team "the Phi Slamma Jammas" because of the way its players slammed and jammed the ball through the hoop. No team in college basketball dunked the ball like the Cougars.

The University of Houston, ranked Number 1 in the nation, met the University of Louisville, ranked Number 2, in the semifinals of the 1983 National Collegiate Athletic Association (NCAA) playoffs.

Hakeem Olajuwon, the Cougars' 7 foot center, began the show. He slapped away a jump shot by Louisville's Charles Jones. Then Clyde "the Glide" Drexler scored Houston's first dunk by going up over Rodney McCray. Spinning his arm like a windmill, Drexler slammed the ball through the hoop. A few minutes later Drexler dunked the ball a second time—over Rodney's brother Scooter McCray.

Despite these thrilling dunks, "the Phi Slamma Jammas" were in trouble. At the half the Louisville Cardinals led 41–36. Midway through the second half Houston still trailed 57–49. Then came what *Sports Illustrated*, a popular sports magazine,

Hakeem grabs a rebound against the University of Louisville in the semifinals of the 1983 NCAA playoffs.

called "the most breathtaking basketball ever witnessed in these championships." With Olajuwon and Drexler leading the way, Houston outscored the Cardinals 17 points to one. Suddenly the score was 66–58, in favor of the Cougars. The Houston team had 14 dunks before the game ended in a 94–81 Cougar victory. Scooter McCray couldn't believe it. "I've never seen anything like it in a real game," he said.

By the spring of 1983 Olajuwon was recognized as one of the finest shotblockers and dunkers in college basketball. In the victory over Louisville, he had 21 points, 22 rebounds, and 8 blocked shots. Teammate Benny Anders said, "The Big Swahili shocked the entire nation." Swahili is an African language. And Africa is where Olajuwon was born and raised. He had learned to play basketball in his native country of Nigeria—8,000 miles from Houston, Texas.

In the next game, if Houston could beat North Carolina State University, the Cougars would be the NCAA champions—the best team in college basketball. The Cougars were heavily favored. After all the North Carolina Wolfpack had already lost ten times in the 1982–83 season, while Houston had been beaten only twice.

But North Carolina State surprised almost everybody by taking a 33–25 halftime lead. Thurl Bailey was killing the Cougars with his long jump shots. He alone had 15 points in the first half. Then Houston exploded, scoring 15 points in a row to lead 40–33. Olajuwon got 20 points before the game was over. Also, his blocked shots helped hold State to only two points in the first ten minutes of the second half!

With 10:04 remaining in the game, Houston led 42–35. Coach Guy Lewis was confident enough to take Olajuwon out for a rest. But as State began to chip away at the Houston lead, Olajuwon went back in. However, there was not much he could do this time. The Wolfpack shooters avoided his long

Hakeem goes high to release a jump shot.

arms by taking outside jump shots that were hard to block. After Dereck Whittenburg dropped a pair of jumpers, the score was tied 52–52.

With a minute left Alvin Franklin had a chance to put the Cougars back ahead. But his free throw missed, and State's Cozell McQueen got the rebound. The Wolfpack controlled the ball, waiting for the clock to run down so they could take the last shot.

With less than ten seconds left, Whittenburg had the ball at midcourt. He looked ready to try another jump shot, but Anders did not want to give him a chance. Anders raced by, reached in, and almost got the ball. But at the last instant, Whittenburg turned away and dribbled toward the basket.

Whittenburg was still thirty-five feet away when he went up and released the ball. Olajuwon moved toward the basket to grab the rebound. If the shot missed he did not want the Wolfpack to get another shot. Olajuwon wanted the clock to run out so the game would go into overtime.

But while Olajuwon was moving toward the basket, State's Lorenzo Charles was moving in front of him. Both players and fans watched the ball arc toward the basket.

Whittenburg's shot was weak. It never made it to the backboard. In fact, it never even made it to the hoop! There would not be a rebound. Charles jumped up and met the ball in the air. Then he immediately slammed it through the hoop. The buzzer sounded and the game ended. North Carolina State had won a shocking 54–52 victory over Houston.

Olajuwon was not the only person who could not believe what had happened. He cried as he walked from the court. Months later he said, "Any time I think of the championship game, I never think about the last minute. I feel too bad just mentioning it. . . . I don't want to feel like that again. It was heartbreaking." Nobody blamed him for the loss. In fact, Hakeem was named the Most Outstanding Player of the NCAA tournament. It was the first time in seventeen years that a player from a losing team had won that honor.

Hakeem Olajuwon was only twenty years old when Houston lost to North Carolina State. He could still look forward to at least another year with the Cougars and then maybe a long career as a professional player in the National Basketball Association (NBA).

"The Big Swahili" was not his only nickname. Many basketball fans called him "Hakeem the Dream." Having a great player like Olajuwon on their team was a dream come true for the Houston fans. But Hakeem's whole life was a dream come true. The fact that he had come all the way from Africa to become an American superstar was hard to believe. And the fact that until he was fifteen he had never even picked up a basketball was even harder to believe!

Hakeem didn't learn to play basketball until he was a teenager.

Chapter 2

More than a 100 million people live in Nigeria, most of them in rural areas. But in recent years, more and more Nigerians have moved to the big cities near the Atlantic Ocean—Lagos, Ibadan, and Oghomosho. More than one million people live in Lagos, Hakeem's hometown.

Since Nigeria lies just a few miles north of the equator, it is one of the hottest countries in the world. The average temperature is around 80° F. It is not unusual for the temperature to hit 100° F any day of the year.

Most Nigerians do not eat much meat. Their favorite foods are vegetables such as yams, corn, rice, and beans. Almost all Nigerian foods are spicy and hot because Nigerians put bits of red peppers in nearly everything.

Outside the large cities, most Nigerians are farmers. They live much as their ancestors have lived for generations. Their homes are made of dried mud, grass, or wood.

Some people in Lagos and the other big cities live in apartment buildings or modern homes like those in the United States. Many rich Nigerians wear dresses, jeans, suits, ties, and such clothing popular in the United States and other western countries. Their lives are much like those of most Americans.

Hakeem Abdul Ajibola Olajuwon was born January 21, 1963 in Lagos, Nigeria. Years later, after he came to the United States, Hakeem was angry about some American attitudes toward Africa. "I know some people think that when

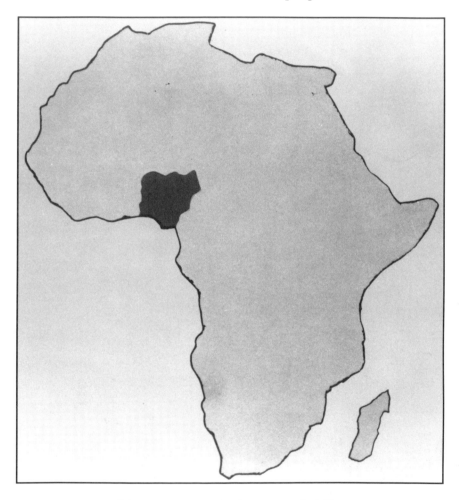

Hakeem grew up in Nigeria, a country in Africa.

I was living in Lagos I was naked in the jungle and swinging in the trees," he said. "And I do not like it. No! I do not like it when TV only shows the bad things and then says, 'This is Lagos.' There are bad things, sure, but in Lagos we have designer clothes, big buildings, videos, and many other things that people enjoy in America. TV doesn't show that, and I get tired of trying to explain that."

Hakeem's parents, Salaam and Abike Olajuwon, owned their own cement business. They had a home of their own in Lagos. Like most other Nigerians they could speak several languages. Before he grew up, Hakeem could speak English, French, and four different African languages—Yoruba, Hausa, Ibo, and Ido. He, his four brothers, and his one sister went to school near their house.

The Olajuwon home was a red concrete house with three bedrooms. The streets in the neighborhood were not paved, and nobody seemed to notice the goats and chickens that wandered about. The animals shared the streets with busy

Hakeem often reminds people that Nigeria has many modern buildings such as this hotel.

15

women who carried long, flat trays on their heads filled with foods such as fried bread and bananas.

Hakeem's father bought cement in bags at the docks by the ocean. Once the bags were brought to a shed next to the Olajuwon home, Hakeem's mother took orders and payments for the cement. The neighborhood was a busy place. Besides the cement business and the food shops, there was a nearby furniture store. A man across the street dyed cloth in huge outdoor tubs.

The Olajuwon family had always seemed to enjoy sports. Hakeem's grandfather was an expert equestrian (or horserider) in Benin, a nearby African country. Hakeem's little brother Afis later became a table tennis champion. Like most Nigerian

A Nigerian artist puts the finishing touches on a bust.

boys Hakeem learned to play soccer when he was young. By the time he was a student at the Moslem Teacher's College, he was a star on the school team. Since he was quick and had long arms and legs, he usually played goalie. His job was to guard the net. He loved jumping out and kicking the ball away from opponents before they had a chance to shoot. "They would go away scared," he said.

Hakeem played soccer at a playground near his home in Lagos. The field there wasn't flat and grassy, but instead was hard and rocky. And the only goal was bent. One day when Olajuwon was leaning against the goal he was spotted by a basketball coach from Lagos State. At 6 feet 9 inches Hakeem was not hard to notice.

Hakeem was embarrassed by his height. People stared at him because of his size, so he began to slouch. He did not want to be noticed. He avoided fights and tried to stay out of trouble with his friends. Because if anybody spotted them, Hakeem was always the one who was recognized.

Guniyu Otenigbade was the Lagos State basketball coach who noticed Olajuwon at the playground. He knew that height is a big advantage for a basketball player. He convinced Hakeem to give this sport a try.

At first Olajuwon did not like basketball. When he discovered that he could not jump high enough to slam the ball down into the basket, he became frustrated and started to cry. "I didn't know how to dunk," he said. "And I couldn't lay it up, either. I didn't know how to use the glass. So I just tried to push it in." In one of his first games, he put up a shot that missed. "I was so mad, I didn't go back on defense. We lost the game. I thought at that time, 'I give up. I don't want to play this game any more.'"

Hakeem had another problem. He had given up playing soccer to work on basketball. But he was not sure he wanted

17

to give up another sport he was playing. At the same time Hakeem was learning basketball, he was also becoming one of the top team handball players in his country. The game is played by passing a small ball up and down the field. Points are scored by throwing it into a small net at the end of the field. Olajuwon's long arms and quick reflexes made him a great team handball player. As he said, "Every time I touch the ball, I score." Otenigbade convinced Olajuwon to join both the handball and basketball teams at Lagos State.

"Back then Hakeem was more famous for handball," said Sunday Osagiede, another coach. "In the national all-sports festival I had an ambulance waiting to rush Hakeem from his handball games to our basketball games so he could help us two ways. He led the scoring in handball, and the rebounding in basketball. Lagos State won gold medals in both."

While he was learning to play basketball, Hakeem first heard about the NBA in the United States. He did not get to see his favorite teams in person or even watch them on television. He had to read about them in old magazines printed in a country far, far away. Hakeem's favorite article was about the Los Angeles Lakers. He liked looking at a picture of their two biggest stars, Kareem Abdul-Jabbar and Earvin "Magic" Johnson. "Those names," he said later, " 'Kareem' and 'Magic,' sounded so cool to me."

Jabbar and Johnson were rich, famous superstars on the Lakers—one of the best teams in the NBA. Jabbar was recognized as the best center in the game. One day he would become the highest scorer in professional basketball history. Johnson, a forward, had just joined the team. As a college player he helped Michigan State University win the 1979 NCAA championship.

Hakeem kept growing and, with lots of practice, his basketball skills improved. Finally his coaches convinced him

When he began playing basketball, Hakeem Olajuwon realized that being tall was a big advantage.

to concentrate on his new sport and give up team handball. Hakeem joined an adult amateur basketball team that played regularly in Rowe Park—a place that was not anything like the Forum in Los Angeles—home of the Lakers. Rowe Park's only court was outside and had an asphalt surface. Bank shots were very difficult because the backboards were tilted.

Hakeem was getting better and he finally learned to dunk the ball. But he still got frustrated. He did not like getting bumped and got angry when the action became rough. The problem, according to Agbello Pinheiro, his Rowe Park coach, was that Hakeem was "too kind on court with too much respect for the opposition." In one of his first games Hakeem was bumped and elbowed so much by his opponents that he walked off the court and quit the team. However, Pinheiro calmed him down and convinced him to come back.

After playing basketball for less than two years, Hakeem was good enough to make the Nigerian team for the All-Africa Games in Morocco. He still was not a great shooter, but he was learning to jump and had become a great rebounder. He was also starting to enjoy the game. Each time he grabbed a rebound, he raced downcourt, waving one finger in the air. "Once I start playing basketball," he said, "I don't play those other sports again. Basketball is a cool game. Cool. Also it is an American game. In Nigeria people admire those things. So I wanted to play. You know: 'I'm cool now!' "

He had become one of the best basketball players in all of Africa, but hardly any Nigerians noticed. African fans saved their attention for popular sports like soccer and handball. Even Hakeem's own parents did not go to basketball games. He remembered the article about the Los Angeles Lakers. He wished he, too, could play basketball in the United States—a country where the sport was popular.

Hakeem knew he was not the only fine basketball player

Nigeria had ever produced. Yommy Sangodeyi was also very good. The two players met at a basketball camp in Lagos. "Hakeem said I was his idol," Sangodeyi said. "This is nothing new for me. I am big in Nigerian basketball. The only trouble is Nigerian basketball is not big."

Sangodeyi was thinking of going some place where basketball was big. He wanted to go to the United States, but because he was twenty-five he was too old to play for one of the major colleges. Hakeem decided he wanted to go to the United States, too. And he wanted to go while he was still young enough to play on a major college team. If he did well there he hoped he could someday play in the NBA.

The oldest Olajuwon son, named Kaka, went to college in London, England. He became a surveyor when Hakeem was still in school in Nigeria. The only Olajuwon daughter, Kudi, graduated from the American University in Cairo, Egypt. The family had always planned that Hakeem could attend college, but they were not wealthy enough to send him all the way to the United States.

"I did not want to encourage my son in basketball," said Salaam, "because I did not know the value." He finally decided the sport was worthwhile when he realized that Hakeem could use his skills to get a college education in the United States. "We didn't know the advantages," his father said. "We didn't know he was going to be a superstar." If Hakeem was good enough he could earn a college scholarship.

Chris Pond, an American working in Africa, had arranged for him to try out for Guy Lewis's basketball team at the University of Houston. Hakeem also planned to visit five other college campuses throughout the United States before going to Texas. All that changed, however, when he got to New York City The day was chilly, and Hakeem was very

Hakeem earned a scholarship and a spot on the University of Houston basketball team.

cold and homesick. "I thought it was too cold for me to live in this country," he said. "I was going to go back to Nigeria."

But then he remembered what he had heard about Lewis's school. It was in Texas, a state that was almost as warm as Nigeria. There were also many other Nigerians already in Houston. Several of them were students at the University of Houston, Texas Southern, and Houston State. If Hakeem went to school there, he would have friends from his own country. Instead of taking the next plane back to Nigeria, he decided to give Houston a try.

At first the Houston coach was not really looking forward to meeting Olajuwon. He might be one of the best players in Africa, but that probably would not be good enough to make a major college team in the United States. "Frankly," Lewis said, "they just don't play basketball in most countries the way they play it in the United States." Besides that, Hakeem was too thin to be a real threat under the boards. Even though by that time he was almost 7 feet tall, he weighed only 190 pounds. And he still did not like to be bumped around on the basketball court.

Coach Lewis did not expect much. "I've had hundreds of foreign kids referred to us over the years," he said. Usually they weren't nearly good enough to make the team. But when Lewis saw Hakeem practice, the coach was impressed. He decided to try to turn the 7-foot, 190-pound kid from Nigeria into an American-style basketball star. Olajuwon got his scholarship and began attending the University of Houston.

Chapter 3

Hakeem Olajuwon had potential, but he still had a lot to learn about American basketball. Coach Guy Lewis said, "I don't care how you slice it. He just flat out didn't know how to play." Before he could learn how to play, he had to get in shape. The University of Houston team played tough, hard basketball. Hakeem got tired after only a couple of minutes of running up and down the basketball floor. Sometimes after making a dunk, his back hurt so badly he had to stop playing.

The first thing Lewis taught Hakeem was to loosen up before practicing or playing. Serious athletes never just run out and start playing. They bend and stretch for a few minutes until their bodies are ready. "I didn't know about this stretching," Olajuwon said. When he began each practice with stretching exercises, his back problems disappeared.

Then Lewis worked on Hakeem's endurance. The new Houston player had to get used to moving quickly up and down the court. It is not possible to call a time out every two or three minutes so players can rest. "I kept him out of games," the coach said. "I wouldn't let him practice until he

Hakeem learned to dunk the ball without hurting his back.

could run." Getting Hakeem in shape was not easy, and the results did not come quickly. "That first year he never did get to where he could play a full game. He actually hurt us in there. You can't play uptempo when four guys are running and the other is dying."

While he was building up his endurance, Hakeem also started building up his body. For the first time he began to work out with weights. He also began eating American foods. One of his favorites was jelly beans! For a while, he ate so many that his Houston teammates called him "Jelly." He also ate lots of other American favorites—steak, fried chicken, hamburgers, and ice cream. Once, just before a practice, he looked out his window and saw a fast-food restaurant. "I opened curtain," he said, "and just knew I had to have something to eat. I love to eat. I love hamburgers, too." After finishing two hamburgers and a milk shake, he headed for practice. Soon he was no longer a skinny 190-pounder. Hakeem weighed 245 pounds. He was now strong as well as tall.

Understandably Hakeem was shy and a little overwhelmed by his new home. "I think he was homesick a lot," said Clyde Drexler, a teammate at the University of Houston. "But we helped him, taught him our ways . . . He watched everything we did. He was a hawk."

There were many things about the United States that confused Olajuwon. For example, once in a restaurant he ordered a bowl of whipped cream, but it was not quite what he had expected. "Excuse me," he asked the waitress, "why is my ice cream not cold?"

In Nigeria it is customary for people to bow when they meet someone. Hakeem soon discovered that people in the United States do not bow. "I mean the man bowed after we just had left him an hour earlier," said Drexler. Olajuwon

27

Hakeem worked hard to improve his strength and endurance so he could play American basketball.

watched his new friends and tried to imitate the way they acted. He soon stopped bowing.

When he first came to Houston Hakeem wore Nigerian-style clothes. His favorite was a colorful *dashiki*, a bright, loose African shirt covered with rhinestones. He kidded his teammates by telling them the rhinestones were really diamonds. After a few weeks Hakeem put away his dashikis. He began wearing American-style clothes.

Besides the food and the clothes, Hakeem also liked the way he was treated in the United States. He was no longer self-conscious about his size. "People in America admire your height and immediately respect you," he said. "It makes me feel real good." For the first time he was positive that his height was an advantage. "I just know that everything I wear is larger than anybody else's," he said. "I'm used to it now."

One of the biggest things about Hakeem are his feet. In Nigeria he wore size 14 basketball shoes, which were tight and uncomfortable. But size 14s were the largest size anybody could find for him. When Hakeem got to the University of Houston he was amazed by the variety of shoe sizes. "The first day here the guy takes me to a stall, and there are 14s all over," Olajuwon said. "Oh, I think I am dreaming." But that was not the end of his shoe problem. As in Nigeria all the size 14s were too tight. Hakeem said he would work out in them for a month or so and maybe they would feel better. "The guy says, 'Wait.' He opens up a drawer and there are 15s! I am dreaming again. They are still tight. He says he will give me 16s! Can you imagine this? I don't know what he is saying. There is a whole room of 16s! I cannot believe this. It was the first time I wore shoes that felt like that. They felt like I had no shoes on at all!"

Soon after Hakeem arrived in Houston, Lewis told him he was going to be "redshirted." That meant he would not play on the team his first year. Hakeem was confused and upset. "He thought the ruling meant he had to sit out for four years," the coach said. Olajuwon almost left Houston for Nigeria. He thought he had been kicked off the team. It took a while to convince Hakeem that he would be playing after his first year.

During that first year Hakeem practiced and practiced. When he made a mistake, Lewis and the other coaches yelled at him. "Awww, I know I sound like Hakeem never did anything right, but he had so much dang potential," Lewis said.

The yelling made Olajuwon upset because he was not used to having people angry at him. "You think maybe you're not

Hakeem discusses strategy with Guy Lewis, the University of Houston coach.

doing something right," he said. "I didn't know what was wrong. He wanted me to do things a certain way." Sometimes Hakeem was so upset he cried. Other times he pouted like a child and refused to speak with the coaches.

"I thought he was getting a big head," Lewis said. Then the coach realized that yelling was not the way to help the Nigerian player. He decided to coach Hakeem differently from the way he coached his other players, who were used to American basketball and American coaches. After his first year Olajuwon said of Lewis: "Now he just lets me play. When I make a mistake, he just claps his hands and tells me to keep playing."

Even though he was not playing on the team his first year, Hakeem was full of team spirit. He got especially excited on game days. "In class, in the dorm, every time we'd see him, he'd grab us and say 'You got to win' or 'I can't wait,' " Drexler said. When Houston played against another team, "he'd sit in the first row behind the bench, holler and cheer us on. He was always running down to congratulate us. And he really liked it when I dunked."

After a year of practice in the United States, Hakeem was ready to play college basketball. Coach Lewis could not wait to see him play against other teams. "I never dreamed he'd be this good," he said.

31

Chapter 4

Hakeem Olajuwon was frustrated during his first season of playing college basketball. He was frustrated because he spent so much time on the bench. Houston coach Guy Lewis had so many other good players that he did not always have to use Olajuwon. Thus, Hakeem played in twenty-nine games, but only started six times.

That season the University of Houston basketball team was good enough to qualify for the NCAA postseason tournament. The Cougars kept winning until the semifinal match against North Carolina. Hakeem watched most of that game from the bench. "Against North Carolina . . . he doesn't start me, and they're coming down the lane shooting layups! I am so mad. I am burning up. Coach Lewis can mess up my mind."

Hakeem finally went into the game, but Houston ended up losing 68–63. Lewis was patient with Olajuwon. There were still a lot of things that the Nigerian player did not understand about American basketball. Despite his time on the bench, however, Hakeem had an impressive first year: 240 points, 25 dunks, and 72 blocked shots!

The Cougars' goal for the 1982–83 season was to win the NCAA championship. "We can go all the way this time," Clyde Drexler said. "You've never seen such a confident team as this one." That was the year Olajuwon finally got to show what he could do on a college basketball court. His shot-blocking was awesome. And the rest of his game was getting sharper, too. In a game against Southern Methodist University, he grabbed 22 rebounds—a school record. His shooting from the floor was very accurate. He made 61.2 percent of his shots. By the end of the 1982–83 season, he had blocked 175 shots, slammed 68 dunks, and scored 472 points!

In January of 1983 he reached 11 blocks in a single game twice, once against the University of Southwestern Louisiana and a second time against Arkansas. Opponents of the Cougars were rattled when they saw Hakeem closing in. They rushed their shots because they were afraid he would slap the ball away. Jim Killingsworth, the coach of Texas Christian University, said it was almost impossible for his players to get past Olajuwon. "Unless we get a helicopter we can't get on him," he said. "It's hard to think about making a shot when it may get stuffed down your throat."

"That's the way I like it," Hakeem said. "I have noticed something about that. The good jumpers are used to going over people, and they think they can do it all the time. It's hard for them to adjust." Hakeem had a goal. "I want to try to block every shot I can." Lewis was happy to see Olajuwon on the court. "I have had some good shotblockers, but I have never had any like Hakeem," he said. "He's the most amazing shotblocker I have ever had or ever seen."

Olajuwon was so good that the fans began calling him "Hakeem the Dream." But he wasn't the only Houston player

Hakeem has long been a popular player in Houston first with the Cougars and later with the Rockets.

good enough to earn a distinctive nickname. There was also Clyde "the Glide" Drexler, famous for his long, swooping dunks. And Larry "Mr. Mean" Micheaux was known for his tough rebounding ability. "I don't take no mess from nobody under the boards," he said.

Olajuwon always worked hard at improving his basketball skills. He began practicing during summers with Moses Malone, a star with the Houston Rockets in the NBA. They played twice a week at the Fonde Recreation Center in downtown Houston. Malone kept telling Hakeem to be more aggressive. "Gotta want that ball," he said over and over. "Gotta want that ball."

Olajuwon tried to follow the pro's advice. "Moses always tells me to be hungry for rebounds and blocked shots," Hakeem said. " 'Eat 'em up.' I can always hear him saying that to me. Moses is a great man." Moses was also a great basketball player. Three times he had been named the NBA's Most Valuable Player. The long sessions with Malone made

NBA star Moses Malone practiced basketball with Hakeem at a gym in Houston.

36

Olajuwon a tougher, more confident player. "I played against a lot of pro players without knowing who they were and holding my own."

McCoy McLemore was one of the former NBA players who watched Hakeem improve. "Against Moses, Hakeem was freer, looser, more assertive, going to his killer move on instinct," he said. "It was like he was no longer a foreigner but a cocky, hip, black, schoolyard dude. Confident. A hustler . . . Moses couldn't take a day off against him anymore. They were two titans. The beauty of it was both were laughing. Moses was so proud and tickled. They recognized they could stop each other while nobody else could. It was a dead standoff."

Playing with Malone taught Olajuwon to be tough, to use his strength on the court. He learned to use his big body to box his opponents out and keep them away from the ball. He became much more aggressive. "I like to get in, take the ball away, and have the other man say, 'Where he come from?' "

Hubie Brown, the former NBA coach of the New York Knicks, was impressed the first time he saw Olajuwon play in college. "The explosive jump—a lot of guys have that once, but this kid keeps jumping and jumping, blocking and blocking. And now we know he can score. No wonder Moses Malone practices against Hakeem all the time. After Hakeem, all our NBA guys are chopped liver."

Since the beginning of the season the Cougars had wanted to win the NCAA championship. Their determination resulted in a conference championship and a berth in the national tournament. When Houston whipped Villanova University early in the tournament, Hakeem made his first ten shots in a row. He also had 13 rebounds, 8 blocked shots, and 5 dunks. In the semifinal game Houston trailed the University of Louisville until Hakeem got hot in the second half. After halftime he blocked 4 shots, grabbed 15 rebounds, and scored 12 points. Hakeem's outstanding performance was a key to Houston's 94–81 victory. Lewis's team was now a game away from the national championship. But then in that incredible title game in 1983, Lorenzo Charles's dunk at the buzzer gave North Carolina State a 54–52 victory.

Lewis, Olajuwon, and the rest of the Houston team had to start all over for the 1983–84 season—without Drexler and Micheaux. Hakeem and Michael Young were named co-captains. "Hakeem is a lot more enthusiastic now, and that's from the added confidence he has," Young said. "He's grown up a lot and accepted the responsibility. When we need to get things done, I tell him, 'Come on, let's go, Hakeem. Let's go, captain.' " Olajuwon was ready for the challenge. "Yes, I know I can do a lot of things better than I did," he said. "This year I am going to do things that I just haven't done on the court."

The 1983–84 season was Hakeem's best at the University of Houston. He had 35 points when the Cougars beat the University of California, Santa Barbara 89–79. He had 25 rebounds when Houston blasted Texas Tech University 86–66. And the center got 23 more rebounds when Rice University fell 72–42. At the end of this season, Hakeem amassed 85 dunks, 620 points, 207 blocked shots, and a 67.5 shooting percentage.

Once again Houston was one of the major contenders for the NCAA championship. Thanks to Olajuwon's 25 points and 14 rebounds, the Cougars dropped Memphis State University 78–71. Hakeem then got 29 points and 13 rebounds to help Houston beat Wake Forest University 68–63. He was such a dominant force in the early games of the tournament that *Sports Illustrated* called it the "(H)Akeem Abdul Olajuwon In-Your-Face Invitational."

The rest of the championship tournament did not go nearly as well for the Cougars, however. The semifinal match with the University of Virginia was supposed to be a walkover. But with time running out, the game was tied 43–43. Virginia's Othell Wilson tried to pass the ball to Olden Polynice, who was alone in the corner. Hakeem slapped the ball away and Virginia could not get off another shot. The game now had to go into overtime. "I was scared," Olajuwon said. Houston was, in fact, in danger of losing. Late in the overtime, Hakeem missed a pressure shot. Fortunately teammate Rickie Winslow grabbed the rebound and dunked the ball for a 49–47 victory.

Houston was lucky to be in the finals for the second year in a row. The championship game was supposed to be a "classic" with two of the best college players facing each other for the first time—Houston's Olajuwon and Georgetown University's Patrick Ewing. The Cougars hit seven early shots in a row and jumped out to a 14–6 lead. It looked like Lewis's team might finally be on the way to a national title. Then the Georgetown Hoyas took off, outscoring Houston 18–4 during one stretch. At the half Georgetown led 40–30.

In the second half Olajuwon picked up too many fouls and had to sit on the bench much of the time. When he was in the game his teammates did a poor job getting him the ball. Instead of passing they were taking bad shots. On the other hand, Georgetown moved the ball well and shared the shots. Hakeem was mad. "They play team ball, the way it's supposed to be played," he said. "We play selfish." Georgetown won 84–75. Again Olajuwon cried as he left the court. For the second year in a row Houston had lost the championship game.

Those big losses were hard for the Cougar fans to take, but they did not forget Olajuwon's accomplishments at the University of Houston. Lewis had seen many great college

Patrick Ewing and the Georgetown University Hoyas met the University of Houston in the 1984 NCAA finals. Ewing went on to play with the New York Knicks in the NBA.

basketball players, but he had never seen anybody like Hakeem. "Hakeem has gotten more publicity than any player I've ever had, or even seen," he said. "Through it all, Hakeem has handled it great. I've never seen anything like this. Everybody wants to talk to Hakeem wherever we go. . . People still can't help but be amazed reading or hearing about Hakeem."

Chapter 5

Back in Nigeria, Salaam and Abike Olajuwon had a tough time understanding what their son was doing at the University of Houston. He had talked with them on the phone twice a week ever since he had left home. When they saw a videotape of a game, they were amazed by the number of people in the crowd. Hakeem's parents found it hard to believe that so many people thought basketball was an exciting sport.

While the Olajuwons might not have understood all the fuss their son was causing so far away, they were glad he was in Houston. "Before Hakeem went we knew practically nothing of the United States," said Salaam. "Since Hakeem has been there, we are sure it is a land of opportunity, a place to make a profit."

The Olajuwons, of course, were business people. They wanted to be sure Hakeem had a worthwhile profession before he came home. Basketball had been good for him. The scholarship he earned enabled him to attend college in the United States. His parents did not realize that in the United States, athletes can earn a very good living playing professional sports. And some of the highest paid professional athletes are basketball players.

Hakeem had only played three years at the University of Houston. That meant after the 1983–84 season he had one more year of eligibility. He also had the chance to leave college to play professionally in the NBA. He had yet to achieve his dream of winning an NCAA championship, but if he signed a professional contract, he would become a very rich man. Back in Nigeria his parents were confident he would make a wise choice. "Hakeem is gifted with a mature mind," his father said. "He will decide. He will make the right decision."

Less than a month after the loss to Georgetown, Olajuwon told reporters he was going to leave the University of Houston to play professional ball in the NBA. The Houston Rockets had first pick of the NBA draft and chose Olajuwon. Hakeem was very happy because he did not even have to move. He could stay in Houston and be a professional basketball player. He signed a contract for $7 million to play six years for the Rockets.

Some people wondered why the Houston NBA team picked Olajuwon. After all, the Rockets already had a 7-foot 4-inch center in Ralph Sampson. Why did they need two big men? Charlie Thomas, owner of the Rockets, thought it would be exciting to have both of them on the same team. "It would be something to have Sampson and Olajuwon playing side-by-side." Bill Fitch, the Houston coach, moved Sampson to forward and gave the center spot to Hakeem. When the two big men were on the floor together, fans called them the "Twin Towers."

For years the Houston Rockets had been one of the worst teams in the NBA. During the 1983–84 season, Sampson's first, the team had finished last in the Central Division. Thomas, Coach Fitch, and the Houston fans hoped the Twin Towers could turn things around.

In their first game together, Olajuwon and Sampson led Houston to a 121–111 victory over the Dallas Mavericks. After a slow start Hakeem got 22 points in the second half. Sampson added 19 points and 13 rebounds. When the Twin Towers stood together, their opponents had a lot of trouble getting off shots. Bernard King, then a star player for the New York Knicks, said going against Olajuwon and Sampson "is like shooting a basketball into the forest. You know you've got a good chance of hitting a branch."

In 1984–85, Hakeem's rookie year, the Rockets finished second in the Midwest Division. And Olajuwon's 974 rebounds led the league. He also blocked 220 shots and scored 1,692 points for an average of 20.6 points a game. He was selected to play in the NBA All-Star Game.

In the first round of postseason action, the Rockets faced the Utah Jazz. Late in the fourth game of the championship

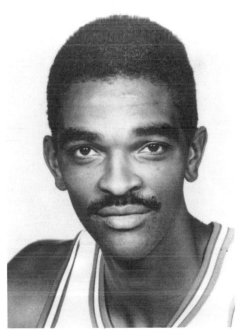

Ralph Sampson was center for the Houston Rockets until Hakeem joined the team.

Bill Fitch was Hakeem's first coach in the NBA.

series, with Houston leading 96–94, Hakeem had the ball. All he had to do was hold it and time would run out, guaranteeing the victory. "I realize I should just hold ball," he said later. "But I shoot it, so I have to make up for it." When his shot missed, Utah got the ball and John Stockton headed for the basket. Olajuwon made up for his mistake by knocking the ball away from Stockton as the game ended. That victory tied the series 2–2. In the fifth and deciding game, Hakeem accumulated 32 points, 14 rebounds, and 6 blocks. However, Utah won 104–97.

The 1985–86 season was Houston's best ever. The Rockets' 51–31 record earned the team the Midwest Division title. In the playoffs the Rockets made it to the Western Conference finals by beating the Sacramento Kings and the Denver Nuggets. However, nobody gave the Houston team much chance against the Los Angeles Lakers—the defending NBA champs. The Lakers still had Magic Johnson and Kareem Abdul-Jabbar, the two superstars Hakeem had seen in a magazine years before. But after losing the first game, Houston won three in a row. One more victory and the Rockets would be in the championship game against the Boston Celtics.

The next game was a brutal battle. Laker Mitch Kupchak guarded Olajuwon. He was rough, bumping and shoving Hakeem, trying to keep him from scoring. Olajuwon was getting frustrated, but he was having a great game. With five minutes left he already had 30 points. That was when the big Rocket center decided he had been bumped enough. He deliberately elbowed Kupchak, who shoved him back. When Olajuwon started throwing punches, the officials separated the two players. Kupchak and Olajuwon were both thrown out of the game.

Hakeem was in the locker room when Los Angeles' Robert

Reid sunk a three-pointer to tie the game 112–112 with 15 seconds to go. With Olajuwon gone the Rockets had to depend on Sampson. As the clock ran down he took a pass, turned, and released what he called a "funky shot." The ball bounced off the rim a couple of times before falling in. Houston had a 114–112 victory.

Now there was only one team left to beat. To take the NBA championship, the Twin Towers and the Rockets would have to beat Larry Bird and the Boston Celtics. Bird was acknowledged as one of the greatest players in the game. He had just won his third consecutive Most Valuable Player award, and he was confident. "I think we're the best team in the league, and the best team usually wins."

The Celtics knew Hakeem was going to give them trouble. "We felt we could not play Olajuwon one-on-one," said Boston coach K. C. Jones. "We had to go make him give it up." He told his players that two or three of them should guard the Houston center every time he got the ball.

In the first game of the championship series, Sampson missed almost all his shots. He got into foul trouble and had to spend most of the first half of the bench. When the game ended, he only had two points. Olajuwon tried to pick up the slack with 33 points of his own, but that was not enough. Boston won 112–110.

Game two was more of the same as the Rockets fell 117–95. "It was our worst game of the year," Olajuwon said. "I was ashamed." Bird had 31 points, 8 rebounds, and 4 steals. He also guarded Hakeem, holding the big man to only four points in the second half. Olajuwon was impressed by the Celtic superstar. "He's the greatest player I've ever seen."

Many fans did not see how Boston could be stopped. Reporters asked Hakeem if he thought the Celtics would sweep the series, four games to none. "Ha, that's a joke," he answered. "That would be a very big joke. I can't believe you are really serious to even ask me that question." After the first two disastrous games in Boston, the series moved to Houston. "I just don't see any way they can beat us here. Now that we're home, in our own building, in front of our own fans, and feeling comfortable. No way."

The Rockets trailed in the third game 76–65, but battled back to take a 103–102 lead with 1:07 remaining in the game. Danny Ainge dropped in a jump shot to regain the lead for the Celtics. Then Olajuwon got the ball and shot it. He missed, but Mitchell Wiggins put in the rebound and Houston now led 105–104. With less than ten seconds to go Robert Parish missed a shot for Boston and the referees called a jump ball—Sampson against Parish. Sampson tipped the ball to Olajuwon, who was immediately fouled by Bird. Hakeem made the free throw, putting the finishing touches on a 106–104 Rocket win.

Larry Bird was already recognized as one of the NBA's finest players when he and the Boston Celtics met the Rockets in the 1986 NBA finals.

Now the Rockets were the ones who were confident. "We haven't played to our potential," Olajuwon said. "We can play a lot better." But in the fourth game, once again, Bird proved too much. With the game tied 101–101, he dropped in a three-pointer. Boston won 106–103 and now led the series 3–1. One more loss and the series was over for Houston.

Olajuwon and the Rockets did not quit, however. They surprised Boston 111–96 as Hakeem sunk 32 points, grabbed 14 rebounds, and blocked 8 shots. Two more victories and they—not the Celtics—would be champions. An NBA title would mean a lot to Olajuwon. He had come so close at the University of Houston to winning the NCAA championship. This time he wanted to go all the way.

Early in the sixth game he was all over the court. Three times in a row he stole the ball from Boston's Bill Walton. He turned two of the steals into slam dunks. That made Bird mad. The Celtic superstar started shouting at his teammates, trying to fire them up. "Just by getting mad and storming around, I got everybody's attention," Bird said. "I didn't want this day to slip away from me." The Celtics responded by making the big shots and covering the "Twin Towers" like glue. "I don't remember the last time I was hounded by a team more than I was today," Sampson said. "Every time I touched the ball, there were two and three guys around me. And that went for Hakeem, too." Boston won the game 114–97.

Once again Hakeem went home to Houston without a championship. But basketball fans expected to hear a lot more from him. After all he was only twenty-three, and already he had played for three championships— two for the Cougars in the NCAA tournament and one for the Rockets against the Celtics in the NBA. *Sports Illustrated* predicted more great seasons for the Rockets. "Say this for the Houston Rockets," the article read. "They are the team of tomorrow."

The loss in the NBA finals was a big disappointment for Hakeem and the rest of the Houston Rockets.

Chapter 6

When Hakeem Olajuwon came to the United States in 1980 his parents figured he would get his college education. Then he would come home to Nigeria and help out with the family cement business. But four years later Hakeem had left college to become a millionaire professional basketball player. He did not have to worry about the cement business anymore. Two years after the first contract, he signed a second one that would pay him $20 million over the next ten years. He was only twenty-three years old, but he was making $2 million a year.

Olajuwon studied business and finance in college, so he made a lot of his own decisions about how to invest his money. He had fun with some of it. He wore expensive designer clothes and drove a fancy car with a personalized "DREEM" license plate. He also purchased many paintings for his home in Houston. Sometimes people were surprised by his interest in the stock market, fashion, or art. Olajuwon said, "When you use your brain to excel in something which is apart from your primary field, there's a real feeling of accomplishment."

Basketball, of course, remained his number one interest, and he still loved playing. "It's the movement," he said. "There's a feel to it. When you shoot it, and you make the basket, it's just a good feeling." He enjoyed going against other great players. "Once I get into the game I get carried away," he said. "I don't think about anything else. There's pressure, but there's also competition. I look at it as a challenge, and I don't mind a challenge."

In his first six years as a professional, Hakeem was selected every season to play in the NBA All-Star Game. Only an injury finally kept him out in 1991.

After Olajuwon led the Rockets to the NBA finals in 1986, he had another fine season. In that 1986–87 season he blocked 254 shots and scored 1,755 points. But Houston only made it to the second round of the playoffs before losing to the Seattle Supersonics.

The 1987–88 season was a rough one. Houston was

Ralph Sampson was traded from the Rockets to the Golden State Warriors after the 1987–88 season. Later he played for the Sacramento Kings.

knocked out in the postseason playoffs by the Dallas Mavericks, three games to one. After that Coach Bill Fitch was replaced by Don Chaney. By that time one half of the Twin Towers was gone. Ralph Sampson had been traded to the Golden State Warriors. "I was surprised," Olajuwon said. "I didn't think Houston would do that. But if you look at it from a business point of view, the Rockets needed a real good point guard and also a strong forward." They got Joe Barry Carroll and Sleepy Floyd. "The Twin Towers were not working out all the time," Hakeem added.

But Hakeem on his own seemed to be working out just fine. He led the NBA in rebounding in the 1988–89 and 1989–90 seasons. During these two seasons he also had his two best scoring totals—2,034 and 1,995—and his two best blocked shot totals—282 and 376. In the 1989–90 season Olajuwon became the first player in 13 years to lead the league in both rebounds and blocked shots.

Bill Cartwright's collision with Hakeem resulted in a serious injury.

Hakeem missed twenty-six games while his eye injury healed.

Chaney, the Rockets' new coach, said Hakeem just kept getting better and better. Late in the 1990 regular season, Houston blasted the Warriors 129–109—thanks to Olajuwon's 29 points, 18 rebounds, and 11 blocked shots. "I don't know if it's possible to play a more complete game than he did against the Warriors," the Rockets' coach said. "He plays so hard every night." In two other games the same week, Hakeem had 41 points and 14 rebounds against the San Antonio Spurs, and 37 points and 25 rebounds against the Detroit Pistons.

Despite Olajuwon's great career, the Rockets were having trouble. The team finished second in its division in 1988–89, but then was eliminated from the playoffs in just four games by the Seattle SuperSonics. The team's record fell to 41–41 the next year. And they lost to the Lakers three games to one in the first round of the playoffs.

Hakeem and the rest of the Rockets hoped 1990–91 would be a great season for them. But on January 3, 1991, misfortune struck. During a game with the Chicago Bulls several players went for a loose ball. There was some bumping as Chicago's Bill Cartwright swung his body around. One of his elbows caught Olajuwon in the head. The big center went down and the game was stopped.

"I was afraid because I didn't know how bad it was," Hakeem said. "I couldn't see out of my right eye. I thought I was blind. On the floor I didn't even know what was going on, I was in so much pain." His eyesight eventually returned, but Cartwright's elbow had fractured Hakeem's right eye socket. Olajuwon was unable to play for the next eight weeks.

While Hakeem was recovering, coach Chaney and the Rockets had to come up with a new strategy. Until the injury they had always concentrated on getting the ball to Olajuwon so that he could do most of the scoring. With their big center gone, they had to rely on a more balanced attack. Players such as Sleepy Floyd, Kenny Smith, and Vernon Maxwell helped pick up the scoring slack. Minnesota coach Bill Musselman was impressed. "They move the ball better and make the extra pass," he said. "They get everybody involved without him." While Olajuwon was gone Houston's record was 16–10.

Hakeem was surprised, but pleased, by his team's performance. "If it took this injury to bring out the best in our team," he said, "then it's worth it." He was also very anxious to get back into action. When the doctors told him his eye had healed, he said, "I'm like a little kid. I get a chance to play again. I'm excited just to be back there."

Chaney and the Rockets were glad to have him back. "We're playing great basketball right now," the coach said, "and we're rolling real good. Now we're bringing back our best player. As far as I'm concerned, we're going to play great basketball from now on." He told the team nothing could stop them. "Now we've got our nuclear weapon back. We're on a mission." That mission was to win the NBA championship.

When he returned to the court Olajuwon worked hard to fit in with the Rockets' new style of play. He did not try to do all the scoring himself. Often, instead of shooting, he passed the ball to his teammates. "Hakeem is sacrificing his individual statistics to help the team win," said Steve Patterson, the Rockets' general manager.

As the team fought its way through the rest of the season, Olajuwon announced a personal decision. Ever since he had come to the United States ten years before, his first name had been spelled "Akeem." That wasn't the way it had been spelled in Nigeria. " 'Akeem' is just the way that many people write my name when they are putting it into English." Olajuwon decided he wanted to go back to the original spelling. "I've decided to put the "h" in the front and make it

'Hakeem.' " In Arabic "Hakeem" means a wise man or a doctor. "Akeem" has no Arabic translation.

However, Olajuwon did not spend a lot of time worrying about the spelling of the name. He was much more worried about the Rockets' efforts to win the championship. "If we take one game at a time and play it with full intensity, the sky's the limit," he said. For a while, Houston was the hottest team in the NBA. After the All-Star break, they won 26 games while losing only 9.

But once again Houston came up short. In the first round of the playoffs, the Rockets faced the Los Angeles Lakers. In the opener, Byron Scott's jumper with three seconds left gave the Lakers a 94–92 victory. Los Angeles won again, 109–98, and Houston was down two games to none.

Then in the third and final game of the series, Olajuwon had 21 points and 17 rebounds. But even this was not enough for the Rockets to win. With 16 seconds remaining Scott got another clutch shot and put Los Angeles ahead to stay. The Lakers won 94–92. Once again the season had ended without a championship for Hakeem's team.

Midway through the 1991–92 season, with a 26-26 record, the Rockets hired Rudy Tomjanovich as their new coach. Houston finished the season at 42-40, failing to make the playoffs. Hakeem had an outstanding 1992–93 season. He was named NBA Defensive Player of the Year and led the NBA in blocked shots.

By the end of the 1993–94 season, Olajuwon had added another award to his list of honors: the MVP. Once again, he helped propel the Rockets into the playoffs. After soundly defeating the Utah Jazz in the Western Conference finals, the Rockets went on to face the New York Knicks for the NBA championship.

The best-of-seven series was a battle between Olajuwon

Michael Jordan and the Chicago Bulls won the 1990–91 NBA championship by beating the Los Angeles Lakers, the team that had defeated the Houston Rockets.

and the Knicks' star center Patrick Ewing. Houston grabbed an early lead, winning Game One, 85–78. But New York came right back, winning the second game, 91–83. By Game Three, the Knicks began sending in a swarm of defenders to keep Olajuwon from shooting. However, Houston managed to squeak by New York for a 93–89 victory in the third game.

Despite the Rockets' 2–1 lead, the Knicks claimed a resounding 91–82 victory in the fourth game. The Knicks also took the fifth game, 91–84, taking the lead with three games to two. They needed one more victory to win the series. But then, the Rockets went to work in Game Six. The game was nearly deadlocked up until the final seconds. When the clock ran out, Houston led 86–84.

In Game Seven, Hakeem led the Rockets to a 90–84 victory, making them the NBA champions for the first time in the team's history. Olajuwon also became the first player ever to be named regular season MVP, playoff MVP, and Defensive Player of the Year.

Hakeem Abdul Ajibola Olajuwon had come a long way from the day in 1980 when he showed up at the University of Houston. Since then he has become one of the finest basketball players in the world. Nearly all the other college and professional players he has faced had the advantage of playing basketball ever since they were small children. "Hakeem was never taught the proper fundamentals of basketball while he was growing up," said Guy Lewis, the University of Houston coach. "He's still become a great player."

A reporter once asked Lewis how good Olajuwon would have been if he had played the game and had proper coaching when he was a kid. "It's so scary you'll never know," he said. "Geez, man alive, he would be something."

Career Statistics

College

Year	Team	GP	FG%	REB	PTS	AVG
1981-82	University of Houston	29	607	179	240	8.3
1982-83	University of Houston	34	612	388	472	13.9
1983-84	University of Houston	37	675	500	620	16.8
	TOTAL	100	639	1067	1332	13.3

NBA

Year	Team	GP	FG%	REB	AST	STL	BLK	PTS	AVG
1984-85	Houston	82	.538	974	111	99	220	1692	20.6
1985-86	Houston	68	.526	781	137	134	231	1597	23.5
1986-87	Houston	75	.508	858	220	140	254	1755	23.4
1987-88	Houston	79	.514	959	163	162	214	1805	22.8
1988-89	Houston	82	.508	1105	149	213	282	2034	24.8
1989-90	Houston	82	.501	1149	234	174	376	1995	24.3
1990-91	Houston	56	.508	770	131	121	221	1187	21.2
1991-92	Houston	70	.502	845	157	127	304	1510	21.6
1992-93	Houston	82	.529	1068	291	150	342	2140	26.1
1993-94	Houston	80	.528	955	287	128	297	2184	27.3
	TOTAL	756	.516	9464	1880	1448	2741	17899	23.7

Index

McCray, Scooter, 7, 9
McLemore, McCoy, 37
McQueen, Cozell, 11
Memphis State University, 38
Morocco, 20
Moslem Teacher's College, 17
Musselman, Bill, 58

N

National Collegiate Athletic
  Association (NCAA), 7-12,
  18, 33, 34, 37-40, 44, 50
NBA All-Star Game, 45, 54
New York City, 21
New York Knicks, 37, 40, 45
Nigeria, 9, 13-18, 20-21, 23, 27,
  29, 30, 43, 53, 58
North Carolina State University,
  9-12, 38

O

Ogbomosho, Nigeria, 13
Olajuwon, Abike, 15, 16, 20, 43, 53
Olajuwon, Afis, 16
Olajuwon, Kaka, 21
Olajuwon, Kudi, 21
Olajuwon, Salaam, 15, 16, 20, 43, 53
Osagiede, Sunday, 18
Otenigbade, Ganiyu, 17, 18

P

Parish, Robert, 49
Patterson, Steve, 58
"Phi Slamma Jammas," 7
Pinheiro, Agbello, 20
Polynice, Olden, 39
Pond, Chris, 21

R

Reid, Robert, 47-48
Rice University, 38
Rowe Park, 20

S

Sacramento Kings, 47, 54

Sampson, Ralph, 44-45, 48, 50, 54, 55
San Antonio Spurs, 57
Sangodeyi, Yommy, 21
Scott, Byron, 59
Seattle SuperSonics, 54, 57
Smith, Kenny, 58
soccer, 17
Southern Methodist University, 34
Sports Illustrated, 7, 38, 50
Stockton, John, 47

T

Texas Christian University, 34
Texas Southern University, 23
Texas Tech University, 38
Thomas, Charlie, 44

U

University of Arkansas, 34
University of California, Santa
  Barbara, 38
University of Houston, 7-12,
  21-23, 25-31, 33-41, 43-44,
  50, 59, 61
University of Louisville, 7-9, 37-38
University of North Carolina, 33
University of Southwestern
  Louisiana, 34
University of Virginia, 39
Utah Jazz, 45, 47

V

Villanova University, 37

W

Walton, Bill, 50
Whittenburg, Dereck, 11
Wiggins, Mitchell, 49
Wilson, Othell, 39
Winslow, Rickie, 39

Y

Young, Michael, 38

64

3